D1592371

Ventriloquism for Beginners

My Partner and I

VENTRILOQUISM
FOR BEGINNERS

A Complete Set of Lessons in the Art of Voice Magic

by DOUGLAS HOULDEN, AIMC

Illustrated by the Author

South Brunswick and New York:

A.S. BARNES AND COMPANY

VENTRILOQUISM FOR BEGINNERS. © *1958*
by Nicholas Kaye Ltd.
First American edition published 1967
by A. S. Barnes and Company, Inc.,
Cranbury, New Jersey 08512

New printings 1973, 1976

3 9082 05411769 5

ISBN: 0-498-06714-9

Printed in the United States of America

Contents

List of Illustrations

THE DIAGRAMS

Details of the photographs appear overleaf

THE PHOTOGRAPHS

Introduction: What is Ventriloquism?

W ELL, first and foremost, it is a form of entertainment. When properly performed it is, like most other kinds of entertainment, a combination of skill and artistry.

The skill in Ventriloquism lies in making one's voice appear to come from someone or somewhere remote from oneself, and at the same time altering that voice in pitch and character to an entirely different one; also in manipulating an automaton or dummy to make it seem to be alive.

The art in Ventriloquism shows in how much entertainment one gives to other people by this 'bringing to life' of a dummy with voice, gesture and personality.

This book sets out to teach you the basic exercises, in simple stages, for developing a distinct voice and character for your 'partner' and then how to combine these in the final performance. New ideas in figure manipulation are explained, also the making or adapting of various accessories. Dialogues are included and many hints given for writing your own material.

The 'Distant Voice' is fully dealt with, together with ideas for its use, and the book concludes with a chapter on 'Novelties', with practical directions for making many of them yourself.

Matthews' News and Photo Agency

The late well-loved Fred Russell is called 'the Father of Modern Ventriloquism' because he was the first to create a real character for his partner, 'Coster Joe'. Here is a photograph of them taken in their dressing-room at the London Palladium. Fred Russell is usually credited with being the first ventriloquist to use a knee-figure. There is however a photograph proving that Fred Neiman used a knee-figure as far back as 1892 in the show of Professor Anderson, the famous 'Wizard of the North'.

CHAPTER 1

All About Me

VENTRILOQUISM as an entertainment is as popular now as it ever was and Television has introduced new ventriloquists to a much wider public. Very many boys and girls are interested in puppets, and ventriloquism is a special kind of Puppetry.

I first started ventriloquism when I was about seven years old, so I feel that much of what I have to say will be a help and guide to young people who are anxious to learn the art.

As a child I was sometimes taken, for a treat, to a variety theatre where, in those days, ventriloquists were often 'top of the bill'. The Great Coram—finely dressed as an officer of the Guards—had a whole stage setting representing White-hall and his partner 'Jerry' was a private soldier.

Arthur Prince was another whose name was known to everyone. He was a naval captain and 'Jim' a soldier. They acted in a wonderful set depicting the deck of a battleship.

Then there was Johnson Clark—the Sportsman Ventrilo-quist. The scene was a gypsy camp in the woods, a hedge and a real stile. 'Hodge' was sitting asleep on a tree stump. Johnson Clark, dressed as a country squire and carrying a gun, climbed over the stile to make his entrance. Hodge's rustic voice made a fine contrast to Clark's cultured tone. Incidentally the stile was made by Professor D'Alvo who gave me some lessons and made my first real partner.

In early days ventriloquists often used a whole stage full of figures and went from one to another giving an exhibition of skill in voice-changing. Fred Neiman presented a Court scene, and dressed as a jester he moved around working each character in turn. At another time he had a minstrel troupe and worked them all by remote control.

12

Arthur Prince
and
Jim

Johnson Clark and Hodge

The idea of trying ventriloquism came to me after seeing Coram for the first time. It was nearly Guy Fawkes' day and I had made a splendid Guy with a papier-mâché face. It was much too good to burn and using some elastic, cloth hinges and some wire I managed to make a rather crude moving mouth. Soon I was practising hard and studying from an old sixpenny booklet I picked up on a bookstall.

An aunt of mine who entertained quite a lot encouraged me to put on little shows for her friends. My cousins had a clockwork figure of a clown standing some two feet high, with a concealed musical box. When wound up he would roll his eyes, clap his hands, shrug shoulders and, I am afraid, poke out his tongue. He came originally from the nursery of the Duke of Northumberland's children.

When the clockwork broke down my aunt had him altered for me by the Professor D'Alvo I told you about. This was the nicest birthday present I ever had. I called him Charlie.

Once, on holiday at a farm—I had had to leave my beloved Charlie at home—I collected some chicken feathers and made a parrot, with which I entertained village children in the barn. The stage was a big corn bin and I also ran 'Talent Competitions' with children from the audience. Make-up in the form of burnt cork was available for my 'discoveries' and the prizes were windfall apples!

I found out, years afterwards, that Laurence Glen, a very fine professional ventriloquist, also used a talking parrot. I have often thought of reviving this idea, but many have done it since and I have never been able to make or have one made well enough to please me.

Incidentally, you may have noticed that I never refer to my partners as dummies, dolls or figures. In my household they are always known by their Christian names and to me they are real people. Only in this way can I convince others that they are alive. They are never left lying about back-stage but sit on chairs and wait patiently until I am ready for them.

A great advantage of learning when young was that my voice never 'broke' in the true sense. My own voice now is rather deep but Charlie's treble is still there and when at the end of our act my partner sings I join in with him. I'm rather proud of this.

That's quite enough about me, but I have told you all this in the hope that it may help and encourage you to make a start.

Terry Hall and Lenny the Lion

CHAPTER 2

Making a Start: Breathing, Hand Exercises, Sounds

BREATHING

J UST as a singer has voice training, and finger exercises are a prelude to mastery of the piano, so in ventriloquism voice, hand and lip exercises are the first step in your training. You can start these right away, even if you have to wait for a birthday or Christmas before you get your ventriloquial partner.

I will deal with breathing exercises first and then describe a very simple gadget which will strengthen your hand for its task.

To be a ventriloquist you will have to talk for two or perhaps more people and, in a sense, you must breathe enough for two. That brings us to Deep Breathing and Voice Control or how to take a big breath and make it last.

This sounds a tall order but I assure you that this breathing will be very good for you and will give you a much richer ordinary speaking voice as well as helping your ventriloquism.

First I must tell you never to make hard work of this. You cannot give a happy performance to others unless you are comfortable yourself.

Now stand quite relaxed and put your hands on your stomach just below your ribs. Take a nice slow deep breath in—and—out without moving your shoulders . . . Did your hands move out when you breathed in? If they did you are lucky and have already got into the habit of using all your lungs and your diaphragm to pump them. Practise this for a few minutes but not too long at first.

The word 'ventriloquism' comes from two Latin words, **venter** meaning **belly** and **loqui** meaning **I speak.** This is what you must learn to do; push air with your stomach or diaphragm up through your lips.

You will all know how a church organ sounds. The rich vibrant tones and thrilling base notes are made by compressed air being released and pumped through the pipes. Large pipes, using more air, give a deeper and fuller sound than do smaller ones.

I tell you all this because I do want you to get your breathing right first of all. So get some good fresh air from your window first thing in the morning and practise moving those hands on your diaphragm. Do it again when you go to bed just for a few minutes before you sleep. After a few days you can do this at any time, going to school or anywhere but perhaps you had better not hold your hands on your stomach! Anyway, you will know by this time if you are doing it correctly.

If you persevere with this you will soon find yourself breathing properly always with no effort at all.

HAND EXERCISES

This photograph shows you what a ventriloquial head looks like when taken out of the body. The shaft is held with the hand so that the head can be turned and the levers which work the various movements can be manipulated by the thumb and fingers. Springs in the head pull the levers up again.

Your thumb will have most of the work to do and at first this will be quite tiring. Now I am going to describe the simple gadget which will exercise your thumb until you get the real thing.

All you need is a piece of broomstick about twelve inches long. It should be just thick enough for you to hold comfortably in your hand.

A ventriloquial head

Now tie to one end a piece of doubled thin elastic so that the loop hangs about halfway down the shaft.

Hold the shaft in your fist and put your thumb through the loop as I have shown in my sketch.

Now if you pull your thumb up and down, stretching the elastic and sometimes turning the shaft by bending your wrist, it will give the same action you will need later to work the head of your partner.

You can use this device later when I teach you some speaking exercises; it might not always be convenient to have your partner with you when you want to practise.

Now let's get back to voice exercises. We have been learning to breathe in deeply and exhale slowly. Now while we are breathing out we will add a musical note.

Sing 'ah' in your normal voice. Your lips should be slightly parted but not wide open. Next sing 'ah' an octave higher but this time bring the tip of your tongue down below your bottom teeth.

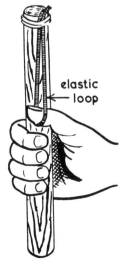

elastic loop

Fig. 1. Hand-Exerciser

This arches your tongue, pushes the sound further back in your throat and sends more air through your nasal or nose cavity.

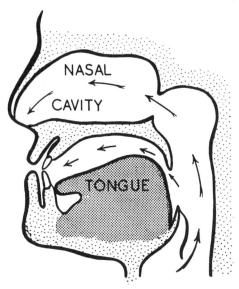

Fig. 2. Directing air through the nasal cavity

This is your first ventriloquial sound and this is the voice you will use when you make your partner seem to talk.

It will not be a nasal sound. Funnily enough a nasal voice is a voice made when the nose passages are blocked, as with a head cold.

You must do this exercise as before, when you get up in the morning and again at night and at any time when you won't be a nuisance to anyone. It should never be much more than a whisper especially at first.

LIP PRACTICE

Up to now the exercises may have seemed a little tedious but now we are going to have more fun. At least we shall seem to be getting somewhere. I expect you have a mirror in your room and you will need this quite a lot for some time. We have now to learn to say the other vowel sounds and watch

Fig. 3. Lips saying vowels

our lips in the mirror because they must not move. You can say 'ah' with your lips only slightly parted and in the mirror they will look closed. Now try 'ee' . . . This will be quite easy and then you can try 'ah—ee—ah—ee' until your breath runs out.

Next try 'ah—ee—oh—ay' all with no lip movement. Don't try to rush things. It may take several days or even weeks to master this.

The most difficult vowel sound is 'oo' because your lips will want to pucker and form a little round hole like this . . .

Fig. 4. Lips saying 'oo'

but if you try hard, watching your lips in the mirror, you will manage to make this sound without moving them. When you've mastered this, try it with the other vowels:

'ah—ee—oh—ay—oo'
'ah—ee—oh—ay—oo'

Persevere with this until you have perfected it and then we shall learn to say the consonants.

LEARNING THE CONSONANTS

If you go slowly through the alphabet with your lips just parted and watching your mirror you will find that the letters that bother you most are B, F, M, P and V.

With these letters either your lips will move or the sounds will not be distinct. They are called *labials* because they are made with the lips.

The old time ventriloquists used to get over this problem in two ways. One was by using a slight lip movement. Even the Great Coram sometimes had a funny little twitch to his military moustache when saying a 'B' or a 'P'.

The other way was to substitute other letters. All the old books advised using a 'G' for a 'B' so that 'Bread and butter' sounded like 'Gred and gutter'. In fact in old-time professional slang ventriloquists were known as 'Gred and gutter merchants'!

This may have been accepted when working at a distance on a variety stage but nowadays we often have to perform close to people and we must learn better ways of making these labial sounds.

Since the lips cannot be used my method is to use the front part of my tongue as this is the nearest substitute for my lips and gives particularly clear enunciation.

We will start with the two easiest ones, F and V. Most people make these with their top teeth and bottom lip. Try saying them normally.

Now, to make them without our bottom lip we will use the tip of the tongue instead. Put the tip of your tongue on the edge of your top teeth and hiss. With a little practice you will make an 'F'. Pull your tongue away smartly with less hiss and soon you will master the 'V'.

Now try F—V—F—V. Here is a tongue-twister or shall we call it 'tongue-trainer'?

'Very few folk forget the view!'

Practise saying this very slowly at first and keep on at it until your tongue gets really agile. This will be enough to go on with for a while, and in the next chapter we shall learn the rest of the labials.

CHAPTER 3

Learning More Labial Sounds

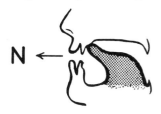

THE next letter we have to learn is 'M'. This we get from the letter 'N'; at least, it has the same vocal sound but it is changed by the position of the tongue. If you can follow my mouth sketches you will see in the top drawing how your tongue makes an 'N'. The tongue is shown shaded. Try it for yourself.

The next drawing shows how by pressing more of your tongue harder against the roof of your mouth you can make an 'M'. Have you got it?

Try saying ... 'N—M—N—M' ... tip of tongue, flat tongue, tip of tongue, flat tongue.

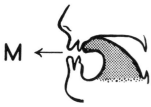

When you can hear a real difference between the two letters try this sentence slowly:

'No more money and not much news.' This will teach you to change quickly from the tip of your tongue to the flat part.

FIG. 5. How to say N and M

Don't forget your deep breathing all this time, will you? The progress you make now will depend on how well you have practised your earlier breathing exercises.

You will notice how these letters are getting more difficult, so don't try to rush things at this stage. Check up on what you have done so far with this sentence:

'Very few men named Michael'

and also—

'Find every man a violent manifesto.'

The last two labial sounds 'P' and 'B' are the most difficult of all, and you cannot take too much care with them. Remember that your skill as a ventriloquist will be judged on the clearness with which you pronounce these letters, and although skill is by no means everything in entertainment, it goes a long way.

My sketches show you the difference between 'T' and 'P'. Notice that when you say 'T' the tip of your tongue presses against your top teeth with a little explosion, almost.

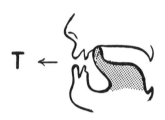

Now press your tongue flat against your top teeth and palate so that the tip curls down and say 'T' this time with much less explosion.

After several tries it will begin to sound like a 'P'.

This is the sentence to practise when you think you have mastered the above exercise:

'Try to pick ten peaches.'

The letter 'B' is formed from the letter 'D' and once again I have tried to help you with tongue drawings. 'D' is made with the tongue tip pressed against the roof of your mouth just above your teeth and then pulled away. Try it.

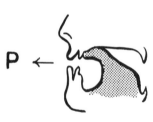

Fig. 6. How to say T and P

Now, 'B' is made with much more of your tongue pressed against the roof, as the second sketch shows. You will have to press quite hard with your tongue and its tip will be further down your top teeth.

If it does not seem to come right at first it is probably because you are still moving the very tip of your tongue instead of the whole front part. All mouths and tongues are not quite the same and it may take some experimenting on your part to perfect it. Keep trying it in various positions until you hit on it, then you will have mastered the most difficult letter.

Be very careful not to practise too long at first. 'Little and often' is the rule here. As soon as your tongue feels tired, give it a nice long rest. This next sentence is not only a tongue-trainer, it is a reminder to you:

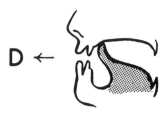

'Don't be difficult, bide your time.'

Before going any further I want you to go back over all the previous lessons with this little sentence:

'Find Ventriloquism by patient means.'

When you can say this while looking in your mirror so that other people can understand exactly what you are saying, you will have overcome the hardest obstacle.

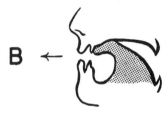

Fig. 7. How to say D and B

You have worked hard and you deserve a little more fun, so try singing that lovely song from *Oklahoma*:

'Oh! what a beautiful morning,
Oh! what a beautiful day . . . .'

First sing it in your normal voice and then higher, in your assumed ventriloquial voice. Then try one line in each voice. This song will give you very good practice with your labial sounds. Don't forget your mirror, but don't rely on it too much. Ask someone to check whether your lips are moving when you are away from your mirror. They may be.

LOOKING AHEAD

Now is the time to start thinking about what sort of character you are going to create for your future partner. It must be quite distinct from your own and the more different you can make him or her in every way, the better effect you will produce.

If you learn to speak a different dialect, this will be a great help. I know many young people are excellent mimics by the ease with which they can 'take off' radio and television personalities, so it should not be difficult for you to listen carefully when a dialect is spoken and to imitate it. I don't mean, of course, to copy other acts but to try and listen to the real thing.

For example, a London boy might like to try a Dorset or Somerset accent, or a Scot could try Cockney. You must remember, however, that your partner will play the lead in your act and usually have the best lines. **His voice and personality should be richer and stronger than yours.** That internationally famous ventriloquist, Edgar Bergen, is not so well known as his partner Charlie McCarthy. Bergen is, or seems, quite a shy person while Charlie has all the cheek in the world.

However you decide, give it plenty of thought now and this will help you later when you come to choose your partner.

Edgar Bergen and Charlie McCarthy

CHAPTER 4

Choosing Your Partner

THIS is a most important step as he is going to cost quite
a lot of money. The most popular partner is the cheeky
boy. He is called a 'knee-figure' as he is small enough
to sit on your knee. Then his head will be nearly on a level
with yours and of course he will not be so bulky to carry as a
full-sized figure.

Don't be tempted to buy a head with too many movements, even if you can afford it. Many fittings are quite unnecessary, in fact they spoil the natural illusion you want to
create. All you really need are Moving Bottom Lip, Moving
Top Lip and Turning Eyes. If you want other movements
like Winking or Shutting Both Eyes, the dealer can have
these put in for you as you need them or can afford them.

If you are fairly skilful with your hands you will have no
difficulty in making a body. It is quite difficult to make a
head, but some guidance in making a wooden head is given
on pages 53 and 54. If you would prefer to make a papier-
mâché head, a book entitled *Fun with Paper Modelling* by
G. C. Payne, and also published by Kaye & Ward, will
help you.

Although it is possible to have a head made to your own
pattern it is very costly. You can, moreover, make quite sur-
prising alterations by re-painting a stock head just as an actor
changes his appearance with stage make-up. You can make
the complexion ruddier for a country lad, for instance, or
paler to suit a town boy. Altering the position of the eyebrows will also change the expression very effectively.

Have a chat with the dealer when you are looking for a
head. He will be very glad to arrange for any slight changes
you may want in a standard head, and you may find it is
quite unnecessary to think of getting something made
specially.

You may be able to buy a second-hand figure, which will be much cheaper. It will probably have an old-fashioned lip movement which shows gaps in the chin. Newer heads have the chin and upper lip made of kid leather and show no join at all. They look very natural indeed.

Please do not think I am implying that you cannot give a good performance with an older type of moving mouth. Some very famous ventriloquists are still using them; their partners are so well known to the public that it would be foolish to change even if they wanted to.

If you start off with an old type of head you should, I think, aim to buy a newer one later if you want to get the greatest effect of realism. Then with the special mouth manipulation I shall teach you, your partner will really seem to be alive.

Another thing to watch for is how the strings are fitted. Sometimes they run through holes in the neck to connect with the various movements. When they break it always seems to be inside the head where they rub and it needs a major operation to repair them. The better kinds of head have connecting wires ending in loops just below the neck. Strings are attached to the loops and can easily be replaced when they wear.

I have found the best string to use is the kind sold as 'chalk-line'. This you can buy at most tool shops or builders' merchants. It is hard wearing and does not stretch, which would throw your adjustments out.

Sometimes the strings have rings on them for your fingers but usually they are attached to levers. Levers are better as you can always find them quickly while loose strings are apt to twist and tangle. They are easy to make and I have drawn two types, one of stiff wire and one of strip metal such as

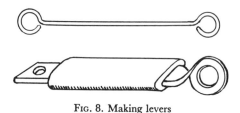

Fig. 8. Making levers

brass. I use the strip kind for the bottom lips and wire for the others. A short piece of rubber tubing pushed over the strip makes it more comfortable in use.

My next drawing shows you how to fix them with screws on to the shaft. The positions must be just right for you and it

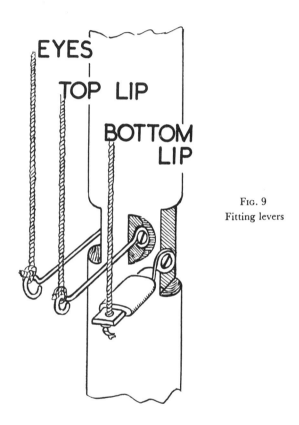

Fig. 9
Fitting levers

is worthwhile taking a little trouble over this. You can experiment by bending the levers and adjusting the length of the strings until everything is made to measure. You may find the levers already fitted in this position; it is quite a usual arrangement. If you go to any one of the dealers listed at the end and mention this book he will be pleased to supply a head fitted as I have recommended.

SUSPENDING THE HEAD

There are several ways of doing this but I suppose the most common method consists of fitting a shelf across the body with a hole into which the bottom of the head shaft fits. This does not give enough flexibility of movement for me, since one is limited to a turning movement only. This is how I do it.

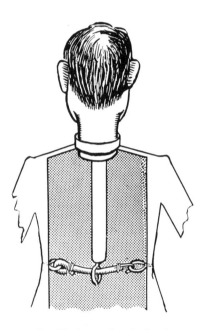

Fig 10 Suspending the head

Into the bottom of the shaft I fix a large screw-eye and two more are fixed on either side of the body. The proper height for them must be found by trial and error. Next I obtain a piece of strong rubber cord; you may find that several strands of model aeroplane elastic will answer the purpose. It must be strong enough to take the weight of the head without sagging. One end is looped through one screw-eye and bound securely and on the other is fixed a small but strong wire hook which passes through the screw-eye on the shaft and hooks into the opposite one fixed into the body. The length of the cord has to be such that, when hooked across, it is of sufficient tension to hold the head at the right height.

You can remove the head when you want to simply by unhooking the cord. With this method of suspension you can move the head into any natural position; side to side, forwards, backwards, looking over either shoulder, stretching up, etc. The only thing you cannot do will be to turn the head right round in a circle. Some performers do this; I have never wanted to, because it isn't natural.

USING BOTH TOP AND BOTTOM LIP MOVEMENTS TOGETHER

Most ventriloquists use the bottom lip movement only for speech and keep the top lip for smiling. I think this is wrong. When you speak you use both lips more or less according to the sounds spoken. The only time I use the bottom lip alone is when my partner says the vowel sound 'I'; mutters or whispers.

In the next chapter I want to teach you the basis of my technique. Much will depend on your own practice and experiment in front of your mirror.

Saying 'I'

Looks away, thinking, etc.

Smirking

Shouting, singing or laughing

Talking

Sniggering

Six different expressions

CHAPTER 5

Bringing Your Partner to Life: Dialogues

THIS is the moment you have been working and waiting for; the moment when you first get to know your partner. I wish I could be there to introduce you—instead I must do the best that I can in print.

What will you call him? I expect you have already chosen a name but in this book I shall call him Tommy. You will have tried all the movements and generally played about a bit so now let us get down to serious business.

Get in front of your mirror, put your right foot on a stool or chair and sit Tommy on your knee. You may sit down later if you like but you will find yourself breathing more easily if you stand at first. Put your right hand through the slit in Tommy's coat and hold the shaft as you have learned to hold your broomstick exerciser. Your thumb will rest across the levers as shown in my drawings.

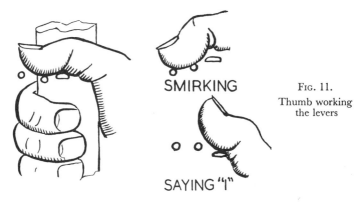

SMIRKING

SAYING "I"

Fig. 11.
Thumb working
the levers

In the photographs opposite you will see some of the expressions you can make on Tommy's face with just your thumb. I hope you will turn back to them again and again as you read through the book.

Now say 'How are you?' in your normal voice and watch what your lips do in the mirror. Try to make Tommy's lips do the same. Don't just give three jabs with your thumb as some performers do. Try it like this:—'How'—lips just parted—'are'—open wider, then closing to make 'you'.

Then try 'I'm very well'. Notice that the bottom lip only moves for 'I'.

Try lots of other sentences, first watching your own lips and then copying with Tommy's.

As I said before, all this is up to you. I can only give you some simple rules. Here they are:

Whispering or muttering—bottom lip just moving slightly. Talking normally—both lips opening slightly for consonants and the sounds 'ee', 'ow' and 'oo';—wider for 'ay', 'ah', 'o'; —bottom lip only for the 'I' sound. Shouting or singing— both lips opened wider, but still varying as in normal talking.

You can see that your thumb has got to be very agile. The levers are like the keys of a musical instrument on which you play the syllables that Tommy has to speak.

The next movement to think about is Head Turning, and here again you will learn most from your own observation. Watch while people are talking naturally and notice how normal head movements are smooth and slow. So here comes another 'Don't'. Don't, except for a special reason, turn Tommy's head with a sharp jerk. This looks more like the movement of a chicken's head than that of a human. Very many beginners tend also to jerk the head whenever they come to a 'B' or a 'P' in the script. They have probably been told that movements like this will distract attention from their own lips but if you have learned to say your labial sounds properly there will be no need for this.

There are of course exceptions. The head may turn sharply in surprise or at any sudden noise, but keep this for special use and generally move the head slowly.

Now let's try some sentences to practise all I have told you so far.

You say: 'How are you, Tommy?'

TOMMY: (slow turn of head to you and away again) 'I'm very well, thank you,' (casually).

YOU: We're going to have a party.'

TOMMY: (sharp turn of head) 'Oo! That'll be nice.' (Tommy gets excited.) 'Will there be cakes and ice-cream and jellies and cakes and ice-cream and jellies and cakes . . .' etc, etc? (until you stop him).

I want you to practise this little piece again and again until you have learned it. It may not sound very funny in print but when you have mastered the movements and timed them properly, I can assure you it will amuse people.

Here is another bit of conversation or *dialogue* as it is called. I shall write 'Vent.', short for 'ventriloquist', when it is your turn to speak.

VENT: 'How are you getting on at school?'

TOMMY: 'Oh!' (Pause—he is thinking. Quick glance at Vent.) 'Er—very well.'

VENT: 'Top of the class?'

TOMMY: 'No. Not *quite* at the *top* of the class.' (Slowly—with emphasis on the words in italics.)

VENT: 'Where then?'

TOMMY (looks away, mutters): 'At the bottom.'

I have given you two little samples. When you have mastered them you can make up some more for yourself, and Tommy is becoming a real person. Remember that variety is the main thing. It is by variety in lip movement as well as change of tone that you will keep your performance alive. Sometimes Tommy will be slow and pause while he thinks out what he wants to say. At other times he will talk in a rush, the words tumbling out. It is this change of *pace* that is so important in any dramatic speech.

You have no doubt had elocution lessons at school and perhaps taken part in plays. This is wonderful training for you. If you can, join a Dramatic Society with a good producer. When you have learned a short dialogue and practised it thoroughly, get your teacher or producer to watch you. He will point out many things you have missed.

When I had been learning ventriloquism for a while I began to speak normally with hardly any lip movement. My elocution master noticed this and showed me how important it was to use my lips well when *I* was talking so as to give greater contrast when my *partner* spoke. I had been so busy watching him I had forgotten about myself.

Another thing you will learn in a Dramatic Society is not to turn your face in profile too often. If you are talking or listening to another actor there is no need to look directly at him. Turning your head half towards him will give the same effect. You and Tommy must remember this and never turn your heads directly towards one another. Tommy's eyes can turn towards you just as yours can turn to him but mostly they should look to the audience. It is not easy to turn his eyes while he is talking and this is a good thing. If you want to do it for any special reason you must learn to stretch your first finger to work the eye lever.

Peter Brough and Archie Andrews

HOW TO WRITE YOUR OWN DIALOGUES

I shall try to give you some hints on writing your own speeches. Not everyone can write well but even if you buy ready-made dialogues (from the dealer who sold you the head), you ought to learn to rewrite them in your own words to suit the characters you have chosen for yourself and your partner. A gag suitable for a cheeky cockney boy may not suit a country lad. So always remember never to change your style to suit a joke however funny it is. Change the joke if possible, otherwise leave it out.

A very good idea is to make a scrap-book of all jokes you think will be suitable from comic papers, bits of everyday wit you hear, and all sorts of sources. Sometimes a very old joke can be brought up to date. Below is a sample of dialogue which came from this old joke:

> BROWN: 'I hear you collect coins?'
> JONES: 'Yes, that's right.'
> BROWN: 'What sort? Old Roman coins?'
> JONES: 'No! New English coins.'

Here's what I made of it. Don't forget you may have to rewrite it.

VENT: 'Have you any hobbies, Tommy?'
TOMMY: 'Yes, I collect coins.'
VENT: 'What sort of coins?'
TOMMY: 'Well, first I started to collect old Roman coins.'
VENT: 'That was very interesting.'
TOMMY: 'Yes, but there aren't many about. I only had one.'
VENT: 'Only one in your collection?'
TOMMY: 'Yes, and that turned out to be an old German coin.'
VENT: 'Hard luck!'
TOMMY: 'So then I started to collect old German coins.'
VENT: 'How many of those did you get?'

TOMMY: 'Just one . . . Same one.' (Pause.) 'So I changed it for an English coin.'

VENT: 'Now you collect old English coins?'

TOMMY: 'No, new ones' (Pause.) 'You haven't got a nice new half-crown you don't want, have you?'

Here is some more chatter based on a central idea. It is about Christmas, but you could write about Sport, Hobbies, School, or any other subject as long as you have a clear idea of how Tommy would behave at these times.

VENT: 'Did you have a nice Christmas, Tommy?'

TOMMY: 'Yes. And lots and lots of food.'

VENT: 'What did you have?'

TOMMY: 'Well on Christmas Day I had turkey, mince pies, Christmas puddings, mince pies, turkey, mince—'

VENT (*stopping him*): 'Yes, yes. What did you have after that?'

TOMMY: 'Turkey, mince pies, Christmas pudding, turkey—'

VENT (*interrupting*): 'All right, all right! I mean for tea?'

TOMMY: 'For tea I had jellies, cake, tarts, jellies, cake, tarts, and jellies.'

VENT: 'And after all that you were full up?'

TOMMY: 'No! After that I had turkey, Christmas pudding, mince pies, turkey, mince—'

VENT: 'You know what you deserved? . . . Pop!'

TOMMY: 'Yes, and a big bottle of that as well.' (*Snigger.*)

VENT: 'Did you have any bon-bons?'

TOMMY: 'Yes, we had a lovely box of crackers. Mother asked me to get them from the top of her wardrobe.'

VENT: 'Well?'

TOMMY: 'On the way downstairs I dropped them and all the toys fell out.'

VENT: 'What a shame!'

TOMMY: 'I had to drop them six times before I got all the toys out.'

This last line was a feeble joke of my own but I worked backwards from it and made up the little story to pad it out.

CHAPTER 6

How to Build an Act:
Mimicry and Singing

You have learnt to perform the little speeches I gave you earlier and have perhaps been able to write some of your own, or at least to rewrite some bought scripts to suit your own style.

Now comes the job of blending all these into a happy and harmonious performance. We have also to think about opening your act and closing it. These are very important points and usually the things people remember most about you.

Tommy, as I said before, 'plays the lead' or takes the leading part and it is up to you to get your audience ready for him. This is called in theatrical talk 'building up his entrance'. If you can play a piano or do any little thing before he comes in it will be a great help in getting the audience in a mood to welcome him.

Whatever else you do, don't carry Tommy in under your arm like a lifeless thing. If you make a body—which I shall tell you about at the end of the book—you will be able to walk him in and his arms won't hang down like those of a rag doll. His head hung on the elastic cord will turn slightly as he walks. I make my partner stop and look all round the audience just by a little jerk of my hand holding his shoulder.

When you perform on a proper stage with curtains, you can if you like get him in place on your knee and be talking away when the curtain goes up, but as you cannot always rely on this it will be better to find a natural way of bringing him into any room.

Suppose you leave him outside the door while you make your introduction. Then you go to the door and call him.

VENT: 'Tommy, I want you to come in and meet everybody.'
(Tommy may be shy.)
TOMMY: 'I don't want to come in, I'm shy.'
VENT: 'Don't be silly. Everyone is waiting to see you.'
TOMMY: 'How many people are there?'
VENT: 'Oh! About fourteen.'
TOMMY: 'They won't laugh at me, will they?'
VENT: 'Of course not. Come along.'

You see how this 'builds up his entrance'. Each little delay from Tommy should make the audience more impatient to meet him.

Then you walk him in to the chair which you have put ready and putting your hands under his armpits lift him up on to your knee. Pretend he is heavier than he really is so that he is quite a weight to hoist up.

Start off quite easily, perhaps asking him how he got to the house, did he have a comfortable journey, and so on. All this is much better and more natural than rushing away with a string of gags. It can still be quite funny; something like this perhaps.

VENT: 'I expected you earlier. Why are you so late?'
TOMMY: 'I missed the 'bus.'
VENT: 'How was that?'
TOMMY: 'I didn't catch it.'
VENT: 'Yes, I know, but why didn't you catch it?'
TOMMY: (*Pause*) 'I missed it.' (*Snigger.*)

Then you may go on with some dialogue, but lead in to it naturally, so that your whole performance seems continuous and not made up of odd bits.

Now I would like to talk about 'impromptu speech', which is speech you make up on 'the spur of the moment' about something happening in the room or about a person present. This is very popular with the audience but of course nothing must be said that will make anyone uncomfortable.

Tommy is always the more observant and draws your attention to things that are happening. All this helps the illusion that he is alive since he seems sharper than you. Many things may happen during your performance and some

you can be ready for by having rehearsed some chatter that
sounds impromptu. There may be a dog or cat or canary in
the room and Tommy will notice these and point them out
to you. You, of course, pretend you hadn't seen them before.

Sometimes when I am performing to children one of them
will stand up, so that others behind cannot see. My partner
notices this and says to me, 'I shouldn't like to be sitting
behind that little boy. He hasn't got a window in him!'
Usually the child sits down at once.

Almost as popular as impromptu chatter is the topical
reference. This is about something in the news or some local
event known to all present. This you can learn before your
act and perhaps give it a comic twist. If you are performing
at school, a kind joke about one of the teachers will go down
very well but make sure it *is* kind and not likely to give
offence.

Other ideas for this type of humour will come to you.
Seasons of the year, of course—Christmas time—pantomimes
—presents—snow.   Summer holidays—seaside—farming—
breaking-up concerts—sports—birthday parties. These are
just a few of the subjects on which you can write lines which
are topical.

WHISPERING

Another little bit of business that is amusing is when Tommy
whispers in your ear. I will describe in the last chapter how
to fit a nudging movement on Tommy's left arm, and this
looks fine when used with a whisper.

I told you how to make his mouth move for whispering,
remember? Just his bottom lip moving very slightly and a
little hissing noise from you.

You might use it like this. Tommy pretends to notice a
little girl winking at him. He nudges you to get your attention and whispers in your ear. You say 'Which little girl?'
and Tommy nods in her direction. 'Winking at you?' Tommy
whispers 'Yes'. 'Well, don't take any notice,' you tell him in
a stage whisper, whereupon he turns to her and gives her a

big grin or, if you have a winking movement fitted to Tommy, he can wink back at her.

COUGHING

This is done by turning Tommy's head away from you (he is polite, of course), opening his mouth and imitating a cough, at the same time giving his head sharp jerks downwards. It may be a little nervous cough because you have caught him out in something, or he may be using it as an excuse to get out of singing a song.

YAWNING

This is rather impolite of Tommy but perhaps you have been talking a lot. His head leans back and his lips open to their full extent. You suddenly notice this and glare at him. When he sees you looking he will stop abruptly.

SHRUGGING

This is a most useful movement when used with the right remark from Tommy. 'I don't care!' he says, and shrugs his shoulders.

You remember I told you that Charlie, my first partner, when he was just a clockwork toy, used to shrug his shoulders? Years later after many tries I made a similar shrugging movement on another partner of mine. It took me quite a long time to perfect, and at last I found a much easier way of doing it. This was far better because I needed no fingers to work it, so that my partner could shrug while he was talking.

This is how it is done. As the head is suspended on elastic you can easily make it jig up and down. To make Tommy shrug you hold the head still and raise the body with your knee. This gives a fine effect of shrugging, as you will see if you watch in your mirror.

SHOWING OFF

I expect you have sometimes seen ventriloquists showing how clever they were by reciting the alphabet and things like 'Peter Piper picked a peck of pickled peppercorns'.

I hope you *won't* do this. In the first place it has been done so often that it is boring. Secondly, I think it is just 'showing off' your skill. This is very proper in a trick-cycling, juggling, or trapeze act but quite out of place in a performance of Ventriloquism.

Instead of saying, in effect, to your audience 'Look how clever I am,' isn't it better for them to say 'We never noticed how clever you were until you had finished'?

I don't think it is praise when someone says to me after a performance, 'I never saw your lips move once'. I always feel that if I had been doing the job properly they wouldn't have been watching my lips but would have been carried away by the acting.

MIMICRY AND IMITATIONS

Many boys and girls are quite clever at making animal and bird noises and imitating other sounds like sawing wood. Here, then, is another novelty you can add to your act. You will find it quite easy with your training to make these sounds without moving your lips and Tommy can perform this mimicry with plenty of movement of lips and head. Make it into a little story rather than a series of imitations. Tommy can describe a visit to a farm—how he was met at the gate by the farmer's dog (dog barking)—heard the chickens in the yard (clucking)—the cock crowed, and so on.

There is no need for me to try to tell you how to make these sounds. Your ears are quick and besides you may learn some new sounds for yourself which will be much better than doing the stock imitations we hear so often. Just listen and copy.

SINGING

If you have built your act properly it should start off slowly, work up to a climax and then quickly finish. One of the ways of providing a climax is for Tommy to sing a song. If your voice isn't too good it should be a comic song, but if your ventriloquial voice is rich and clear there is no reason why he should not sing a serious song. Even if the rest of your act is funny it may still end in a serious mood; in fact this is in the best comic tradition.

I once saw a ventriloquist, I'm sorry I've forgotten his name, whose partner after a very humorous act became serious and sang *Ave Maria* very beautifully indeed. It brought the house down.

Well, you have plenty to think about and practise now. In the next chapter I will tell you how to finish your performance using another trick—the Muffled Voice.

CHAPTER 7

More Advanced Ventriloquism: The Muffled Voice; The Distant Voice; Drinking

I HOPE the title of this chapter doesn't frighten you. You might be thinking that what I have now to teach you is going to be very difficult. This is not so. We have to learn two more kinds of voice, and many people seem to think these are the hardest to learn. Actually they are easier but may be more tiring, and as your partner will usually be out of sight you will not have the movement of his lips to help in the pretence.

In using these voices your ability as an actor will be needed much more, so while they require less *skill* they need more *artistry* to put them over to people.

I shall call them 'The Muffled Voice' and 'The Distant Voice'.

LEARNING THE MUFFLED VOICE

I am going on with this chapter hoping that you have thoroughly mastered ordinary dialogue with Tommy. Don't try to push on too fast at this stage. I know there is a big temptation to learn all you can quickly, but if you try too much at once you may get all mixed up with your voices.

The muffled voice is a very easy and useful one to master, for then you may add another novelty to your act. It all helps to make a change or to add variety. Tommy can be put in a cupboard or a suitcase and keep on talking.

Listen to someone talking loudly in a room from outside the closed door. You will find most of the consonants are muffled. Although the voice will be fairly loud—according to the thickness of the door—it will not be very clear. Suppose he is saying 'Let me out!' What you will hear will be something like 'Le me ow'. The sounds most affected by muffling will be the sibilants. They are the letters 'S', 'F' and 'th' as in *thin*. 'T', which is really a kind of sibilant, will also be nearly lost.

Now, I said this was an easy voice to produce. It is, but if you do it for long it will be very tiring. You have to push your tongue right back in your mouth to throttle back the air, at the same time have plenty of air pushing up from your diaphragm. This will give the muffled sound.

The easiest way I can teach you is to tell you to put the tip of your tongue right down on the floor of your mouth and keep it there. This will lessen the sibilants and T sounds. Now push hard inwards with your stomach muscles and say, well back in your throat, 'Let me out'. Does it sound like that voice you heard behind the door? If not, keep on trying; you'll do it.

When you think you have it, try this little game. Pretend there is a noise from your wardrobe or cupboard and that there is someone inside. Look surprised and say 'What was that?' in your normal voice. Don't forget you are acting a part now. You will be looking puzzled, won't you?

MUFFLED VOICE: 'It's me.'

VENT: 'Where are you?'

MUFFLED VOICE: 'In the cupboard. I want to get out. Let me out! Let me out!'

While the voice is shouting you open the door, and as it opens the voice becomes clear—your normal ventriloquial voice. Shut the door and again the voice is muffled. Practise this change from muffled to clear voice until you can time the change nicely with opening and closing the door.

Next you can try with Tommy by putting him in a suitcase. Here is some dialogue to try.

TOMMY: 'Oo, I do feel tired.'
VENT: 'Would you like to go to sleep in this case?'
TOMMY: 'Yes, I would.'
VENT (*puts Tommy in case*): 'In you go, then.'
TOMMY: 'Shut the lid, then I shan't hear any noise.'
You bang the lid shut and Tommy shouts something so muffled you cannot hear what he says.
VENT (*shouting back*): 'What did you say?'
TOMMY is shouting (*muffled voice*): 'No need to bang the lid like that!' but still you cannot understand.
VENT: 'I'm sorry, I can't hear.' (*Loudly.*)
TOMMY (*very decidedly*): 'No—need—to—' (*you open the lid— clear voice still shouting*) '—bang—the—lid—like—that!'
VENT: 'I'm sorry.' (*Closes the box gently.*)
TOMMY (*muffled*): 'That's better.'

This is a very good way of closing your act. After some such conversation you can say to your audience, 'Well, Tommy is tired and we must go now.' Knock gently on the case and call 'Tommy!'

TOMMY: 'What do you want?'
VENT: 'Say good-bye to everyone.'
TOMMY (*he can't hear*): 'What's that?'
VENT (*louder*): 'I said "Say—good-bye—to—everybody".'
TOMMY: 'Good-bye, everyone, good-bye, good-bye.'
and as you walk out smile, bow and say 'Good-bye' yourself.

I never like to see a ventriloquist shut his partner in a case as a punishment. The poor little chap doesn't want to go in, perhaps he is crying and when in the box keeps shouting 'Let me out!' I don't think this is the right effect to create, certainly not when performing to children. I use something like the above sample, which leaves everyone quite happy including my partner.

Another way to use the muffled voice is for you to clap your hand over Tommy's mouth. I must admit I don't like this very much unless it is nicely done.

Suppose he is making remarks about people in the room and will persist in doing so although you have told him to stop. In desperation you put your hand over his mouth, when he will shout: 'Take your hand away!', very muffled. After this is repeated several times you remove your hand in mid-sentence like this: 'Take your' (*muffled—remove hand*) 'hand away!'—shouted in a clear voice.

This will be acceptable only if it is done lightly, with a smile. Tommy won't be upset by it, he will take it as a bit of fun and smile back at you.

You will soon get to know how much muffling you need to do. You might, for instance, have hidden Tommy behind some thick window curtains before you start your perform-ance. After making your introduction you call to him and he answers. His voice will be slightly muffled but not so much as it would be if he were in a box.

THE DISTANT VOICE

Let me say, first of all, that it is nearly impossible to use this voice in a small room with people near to you. The only way I have ever been able to use the distant voice in a drawing-room has been to call up the chimney to Father Christmas and he answered me. But I only do this for very young child-ren and they *want* to believe he is up there, so perhaps that helps a lot.

In the muffled voice you throttled back the air but pushed hard with your stomach muscles to make the sound more or less loud. In the distant voice the sound, as it has to appear to come from a distance, is softer but it is clear. There is nothing to muffle it. Listen to people shouting from a long way off; that is the sound you have to make.

Start with plenty of air in your lungs and, as in your first ventriloquial voice, hum a note an octave above normal. Now push back your tongue so as to send nearly all the sound through your nose.

Have you ever had a sore throat and been made to gargle? Not a very pleasant subject, perhaps, but it is the best way of describing the action of your tongue, throat and Adam's apple, which is the voice box. Of course your voice will not rattle like a gargling sound because you will have no liquid in your throat.

Now practise this distant note which old books on ventriloquism used to describe as the bee-drone. We won't call it that because your voice will probably be higher than the hum of a bee.

You must keep on trying this note until you get it steady and not wobbling up and down. Perhaps it sounds like a factory hooter a very long way away.

When you have mastered this—don't hurry—I want you to make it gradually louder, then fainter until it dies away. Keep on practising this and pretending it is a boy humming a note riding a bicycle towards you, then riding past and away from you. It will probably feel almost as if the sound is coming out of the top of your head. This means you have got it right and can now go on to words.

Still pretending about the boy on the bike, imagine you have asked him where he is going and as he pedals on down the road he shouts, 'I am going to the shops to buy some toffees and I'll get you an ice-cream.' What a pity it is only pretence!

Practise this sentence, first loud and then dying away in the distance. After that try it in reverse—very faint, and then gradually rising to full volume. You will find that controlling the air coming out will be the hardest part. Don't worry if you find this difficult. As I said before, you will not need this voice in an ordinary room. I expect it will be some time before you attempt a performance in a hall large enough to use it. Many ventriloquists never bother with the distant voice at all.

Now here are a few ideas for using it when you are performing on a stage. You can pretend there is a trap-door behind a screen or curtain and send Tommy down an imaginary ladder to the cellar. As he is supposed to be climbing down you call out to him 'Are you all right, Tommy?' and he calls up to you, his voice getting fainter. Your audience must be able to see your face all the time so that you can help the illusion by your acting. You will show that you are anxious that Tommy should not fall, and you peer down the shaft and shout louder when he is supposed to be at the bottom.

Another way is to pretend Tommy is climbing a ladder at the side of the stage. You walk him off stage out of sight and then come back on stage as you watch him climb. Perhaps there is a slippery rung in the ladder and Tommy calls down: 'Whoops! I nearly slipped that time.' You say: 'Careful, Tommy, we don't want anything to happen to you.'

TOMMY: 'No. You'd be out of work if it did.'

If you can learn to do a gruff voice you can pretend to be calling out to a stage-hand up above the stage. Or Tommy can notice him and call out 'Hoy! What are you doing up there?' and the gruff distant voice will reply to him.

There are many other ways of introducing the distant voice into your act if you should want to. I think I have told you enough to start you thinking for yourself.

DRINKING

Before I finish this chapter I must mention one other feat in ventriloquism, but I am afraid I cannot teach you how to do it in this book. This you may have seen performed. It is the trick of drinking a glass of water while the partner is talking.

I would like to tell you how to do it but I feel that, while not exactly dangerous, it can be very, very unpleasant if some liquid goes the wrong way. I have been doing it for many years now; actually I need the drink before I can make my partner sing his song. Only recently I made a slip and had a very uncomfortable few minutes getting my breath. Luckily I had the presence of mind to keep my partner moving and his face alive so that most of the audience thought it was part of my act. I did not enjoy the applause that followed one little bit!

There is a way, however, in which you can appear to perform this feat. The dealer who supplied your partner will obtain for you a special trick glass, so that you seem to drink quite a quantity of ginger-pop. Actually you drink very little or none at all. You should use a dark liquid like blackcurrant cordial, because water does not show up very well. Having filled the glass according to the instructions given with it, have it handy on a table at your left. Promise Tommy a drink if he is good or if he will sing and he asks what drink it is. When you tell him he says he doesn't like it. Carry on something like this:

VENT: 'Well, if you don't want it, I'll drink it.'
TOMMY: 'What all that? You couldn't drink all that.'
VENT: 'Oh yes, I can.'

You pick up the glass with your left hand and raise it just above your lips so that Tommy's speech will be clear. As you tilt the glass, you appear to be drinking. Tommy keeps talking.

TOMMY: 'That's enough. Don't drink it all. You'll go off "pop" if you drink all that . . .' (*To audience*): 'Look at him. He's going to drink the lot.' (*He watches glass.*) 'Nearly gone—nearly gone—all gone!'

As he says this you put the glass properly to your lips and really drink the little that is left.

Well, I've come to the end of my lessons to you. I could have written much more but I think I have dealt simply with everything you will ever need as a ventriloquist. If, during your practising, you come up against any little snag, turn back and read again what I have told you. I am sure that between the two of us it will sort itself out.

My next and last chapter tells you about some novelties that will be fun to make and fun to use.

CHAPTER 8

Ventriloquial Novelties and Accessories to Make

THESE are not intended to form a complete act but just to be used as an amusing interlude. The Talking Mitten, Talking Hand or a Puppet could very well be used as an introduction before you bring in your partner or it could be brought into your act as a variation. I myself prefer not to do this as I think it breaks the illusion of reality, but anyhow try them out and then see where you can build them into your act.

A TALKING MITTEN

This is a little novelty that is easy to make and great fun to work. It could be used as an introduction to your act before you bring in your partner. I have drawn it full size so that you can trace it.

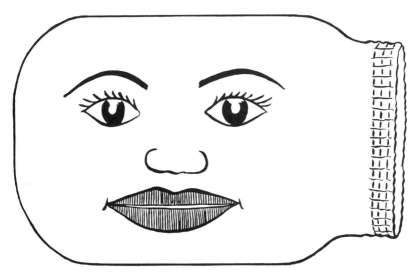

FIG. 12. Talking mitten

The material you use to make it should be stretchy stuff like stockinette. If you machine round the wrist opening with elastic thread it will fit nicely. You could use part of a white cotton sock so long as it is strongly bound where you cut it to prevent fraying.

The eyebrows, eyes and nose are painted in with black ink or paint. The mouth is made like a large button-hole; just a slit which is button-hole-stitched with red cotton to make the lips. If you like you can make a rag body to fix underneath.

To use it you put it on like a glove but double your fingers inside. Your thumb forms the chin and by moving your thumb the lips open in a most life-like manner. The Talking Mitten is something like the Talking Hand I shall describe next, but it has the advantage that it doesn't mess up your hands.

THE TALKING HAND

All you need to make this are two white cardboard discs, two boot buttons, a length of thin wire, some black wool or crêpe hair and some lipstick. Ask permission before you borrow the lipstick!

Cut little slits in the discs and push the rings of the boot buttons through to make eyes. At the back wire them together with a space in between. Now push the rest of the wire between the two middle fingers of your hand and back over the top, down to make a peak and back again to clip over your hand.

Next you must tease out the wool or crêpe hair to form a little wig. This has to be sewn to the top part of the wire where it comes over your hand. Once you have bent the whole thing to shape it will slip on and off your hand without altering.

Now with the lipstick paint in a red nose between your first and second knuckle-joints and paint lips on your first finger and thumb. You can do this in view of your audience,

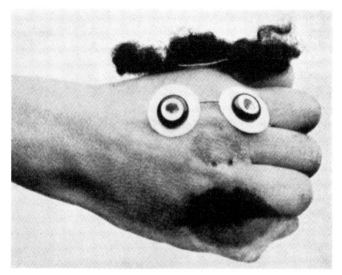

Talking hand

then slip on the eye and wig gadget and you are ready to perform.

Movements of your thumb will give a very good impression of talking. Try it and see.

HOW TO MAKE TALKING PUPPETS

Many boys and girls who take up puppetry make their own puppets. If you are clever enough to carve your own puppet heads you should have no trouble in making moving mouths. Look at Figure 13 overleaf.

When you have carved the head out of wood you must cut away the chin. The easiest way to do this is to cut a slot right through the head as shown in (a), wide enough to take your first finger. Next cut a piece of wood as in (b) and carefully smooth down the sides until it fits loosely in the slot. Bore a hole in the back of the chin part to take your finger-tip.

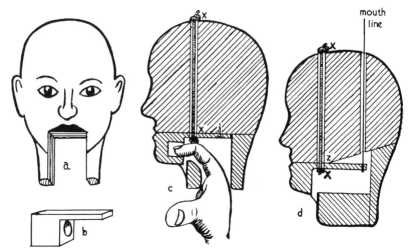

Fig. 13. Talking puppets

Hold it in position in the head gap for the time being with a small wood screw while you drill up through the mouth-piece and through the top of head with an $\frac{1}{8}$-in. drill. (Line X–X in (c).)

Knot one end of some cord elastic and thread the free end up through the hole to top of head. Stretch slightly and tie another knot.

Now you can carve the lower lip and chin, and when you have finished take out the temporary fixing screw. The back and front of the neck should be filled in with pieces of wood so that it will fit firmly on to your first finger knuckle. When the head is painted and a dress and wig fitted on, you will have a very useful actor for your puppet programme.

If you work string puppets they can be made to talk in a similar manner except that the slot is cut as shown in (d). This allows the mouth platform to pivot at point Z. Another hole will be needed for the line which works the mouth. The elastic must only have just enough tension to close the mouth.

MAKING A BODY

I think I told you the first body I made was meant for the Fifth of November. Since then I have made them in lots of different ways, some of which I shall tell you about.

The body must have a hollow chest and a hole for the neck of your partner. It should also be as light as possible. My drawing shows you the correct proportions for a small boy or girl. First measure the head and make the body about twice as long and the legs about three inches longer still. When you fold it up the feet will fit over the shoulders nicely.

The easiest way to make a body is to get a light but strong wooden box from your greengrocer. Cut a hole in one end big enough to take the neck. This should be lined with some thick material like felt to save rubbing the neck when you turn the head. Cut off the two top corners and fix two shoulder-pieces of wood. Then pad the outside with shavings held in place with rag tacked on to the wood.

A further improvement is to find or make a short cardboard tube into which the neck loosely fits. This is glued into the hole and lined and then your partner's collar will fit on neatly.

You might like to try making a chest out of cardboard. It is fixed on the front after you have cut away the wood. It will save padding and give your hand more room to work inside the body.

If you are clever at carpentry you may prefer to build the framework yourself. As long as the sides are strong enough to take the pull of the elastic cord the shape can be built up with thin wood, cardboard and stiff brown paper.

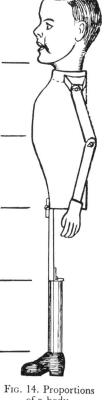

Fig. 14. Proportions of a body

Fig. 15. Making a body from a box

I have given you a pattern of the various parts and my drawing shows how the sides slope inwards at the front. The shoulders slope downwards from the neck, supported at the back by a piece of thin plywood. The front of the chest is made of a sheet of cardboard cut to fit the neck and shoulders. This is securely glued to the wooden framework. The whole thing is then brushed with hot glue and covered inside and out with overlapping pieces of stiff brown paper, or better still, with butter muslin.

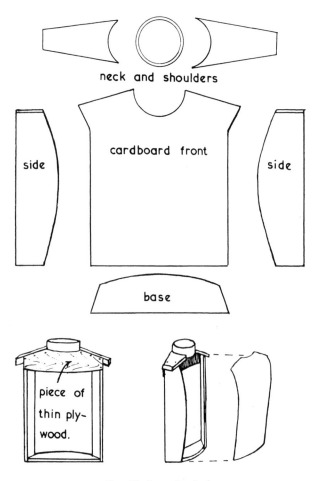

FIG. 16. A wooden body

When the glue is quite dry you will find the body is very strong indeed and will stand up to lots of hard wear.

A BODY OF WIRE

This is very light but strong and is made of galvanized-iron wire which should be soldered at the joints. In my drawing I have shown thick wire for the main cage, and the thin wires merely make the shape. The neck is made from tin which is soldered into place. I have often found a salmon or fruit tin which was just the right size and the top and bottom were easily cut out with a patent can-opener. The tin, of course, has to be lined to prevent rubbing.

The legs and arms are attached to half hinges (X) which you must slip on to the wires before they are bent and fixed. It is easy to knock the pin out of a hinge using a hammer and punch or strong nail.

Don't forget to fix strong wire hooks at the right height to take the elastic cord which suspends the head.

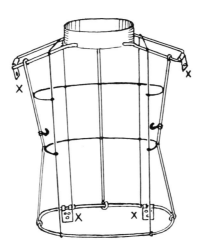

Fig. 17. A wire body

MAKING HANDS AND ARMS

While you *can* use stuffed gloves for hands it is better to make proper ones. You will need two pieces of soft wood each about 6 in. × 3 in. × 1½ in. I have shown you how to mark out the wood for carving a left hand. The right hand will be reversed, the thumb being on the right.

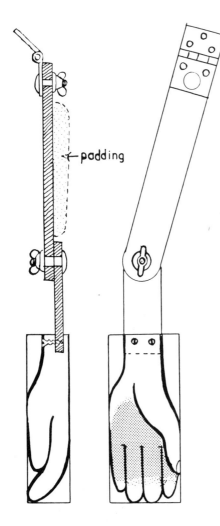

The wood is first roughly sawn to shape then carved with a penknife, rasp and sandpaper. Copy your own hands. In my drawing the part shown shaded is to be hollowed out to form the palm.

After the hands are nicely smoothed they will need painting, first with a priming coat then with a flat paint. Cream paint with a touch of reddish-brown make a good flesh colour. The ends of the wrists are slotted to take the arms which are glued in and nailed or screwed.

The arms are made from 1½ in. × ¼ in. wood and jointed as my sketch shows. Use small bolts and thumb-screws which can be adjusted through the sleeves. Pad them as I have shown. The arms are fixed to the shoulder hinge with one bolt only then they will swing.

FIG. 18. Arms and hands

THE NUDGING MOVEMENT

This is worked by a metal strip drilled and screwed to the arm just below the shoulder hinge. If you push the strip outwards away from the shaft your partner will give you a lovely nudge in the ribs. This you can do with the fingers of your hand holding the shaft as his head will be turned towards you. If you have made a wooden body, you must cut a hole in its side for this strip to slide in.

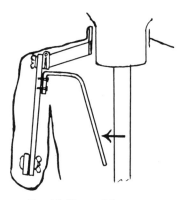

FIG. 19. The nudging movement

MAKING LEGS AND FEET

The thigh parts are made from $1\frac{1}{2}$ in. $\times$ $\frac{1}{2}$ in. wood and the lower legs from $1\frac{1}{2}$ in. cardboard tubes. These you can buy from any good stationers; they are called postal tubes. After cutting them the right length you will need to glue wood plugs in each end of both tubes. The soles of the feet are cut from plywood with a fret-saw and then glued and screwed to the postal tubes.

60

You will see from my sketch how the legs are hinged at the knee and body, although if you have made a wire body the half hinges will be already on the body.

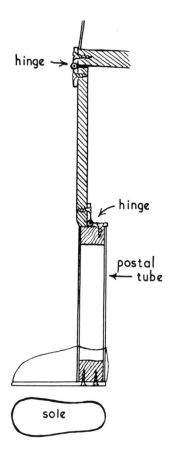

hinge →

hinge

postal
← tube

sole

FIG. 20. Legs and feet

You can fit your partner with proper shoes. They look nice but are heavy. You may prefer to build up shoes on the soles using cardboard and strips of brown paper. After smoothing they will have to have a coat of size before painting them shiny black or brown.

To make your partner walk hold him by the left shoulder. If you now tilt him sideways and forwards, one leg will rise from the ground and swing forward by its own weight. Tilting him the other way will cause the other leg to swing forward also. This takes a little practice but it will look very natural when you have mastered it; nearly as good as the complicated walking movements fitted to expensive bodies.

DRESSING YOUR PARTNER

Here are a few notes on the clothes your partner will need. I hope they will save you from making the mistakes which I did at first. The dress or suit will probably have to be made to measure but some of your old ones will cut down to fit him, or her. Coats should fit well with a slit in the back for your hand. Trousers should be roomy in the seat so that your partner can sit nicely on your knee.

It is better not to have short trousers or a short skirt as it is difficult to make a natural looking knee-joint. For a school-boy you will need a shirt and tie, a blazer and flannels. A girl could wear jeans or a long party dress. Jeans would also suit a boy worn with a high-necked jersey. A Scot would look nice in tartan trousers while a country boy would pro-bably have corduroys or tweeds. Many other ideas will come to you but don't make the clothes too gaudy.

TAKING CARE OF YOUR PARTNER

You have paid quite a lot of money for the head of your partner and it is well worthwhile paying some attention to the way you look after him. Although the head is quite strongly made the outer skin can easily become chipped or rubbed and the leather parts of the mouth are particularly liable to damage. When you are not using him it is a good idea to wrap and tie a padded cloth round his head, and if you find a case or box into which he just fits he will not bang about when you carry him.

His clothes will stay cleaner and free from dust if you keep him in one of those large polythene bags used for storing garments. Keep him in a dry place—damp can do a lot of damage to the springs and other mechanism in the head.

You should always check the various movements before you start a performance and make sure that you replace strings that show the slightest signs of wear. There will be plenty of chalk-line left over which you should keep handy for this job. I always carry some in a box fixed in my case, together with an old razor blade for cutting it. There is also a small coil of soft wire for any emergency repairs to limbs that may be necessary.

With care the head should not need any attention for some years but if a slight touching up is required, mix some flesh paint as I told you earlier, matching his own colour as closely as you can, and apply with a small paint brush. A careful wash with a soapy cloth may be all that is necessary.

Lips and eyebrows may need repainting. Eyebrows should be put in with flat paint to match the original colour. Paint the lips in with glossy red paint and they will have a fresh, moistened look.

IN CONCLUSION

Well, at last I have come to the end of my book but I am very sorry to have to leave you. I have so much enjoyed writing it, and I hope you will have as much pleasure in reading it. I sincerely trust it will guide you well on the way to becoming a good ventriloquist.

And above all I hope you will come to regard your partner as just as much a living person as I do mine. That's the real secret.

Goodbye,

DOUGLAS HOULDEN.

LIST OF DEALERS

L. Davenport & Co.,
51 Great Russell Street, London, WC1
Gamages, Holborn, London, EC1
Hamleys, 200 Regent Street, London, W1
Oscar Oswald, 36 Lexington Street, London, W1

Mr Oswald also has second-hand heads and bodies for sale.